Mastermind Alliance Teams

"Since joining a Mastermind group I have been in the company of extremely talented and experienced people. Because of their experience base, masterful insights into what it takes to be successful have been available to me. Without question, whether experienced or not, everyone needs to be part of a dynamic Mastermind group."
— Don McNamara, President, Heritage Associates, Inc.

"Mastermind groups keep me on track and accountable for my success. My productivity triples when I am actively engaged in one or more Mastermind groups. I've discovered when a collection of brilliant minds, hearts, and talents come together, miracles happen."
— Dr. JoAnn Piña, Professional Speaker

"One of the quickest and most enjoyable ways to get to the next level is a Mastermind group. The accountability and ideas shared are priceless. My goal is to share and learn million-dollar ideas each time we meet, and I have not been disappointed yet."
— George B. Thompson, author,
Millionaires in Training: The Wealth Builder

"Being out on one's own, with responsibilities for providing quality products and services to clients, is often a daunting experience. Joining a Mastermind group has given me the assurance that I will never run out of motivation, ideas, or innovative thinking. The Mastermind group is an indispensable tool."
— Dave Kinnear, CEO, dbkAssociates, Inc.

"My Mastermind group gives me accountability and amazing ideas on which I can follow through. It is also good to have a mirror and feedback from peers. I get things scheduled and accomplished because my group meets regularly, and each week we all have assignments that align with our personal and professional goals."
— Greg Mooers, President, LifeCamp

Other topics in the **Cheetah Express
Professional Achievement Series®** include:

Available in training workshops, keynote speeches,
audio, and/or books.

- Business without Biceps: The Untold Truths of Women in
  Business and How to Make Them Work for You

- Off the Wall: Creative Problem Solving and Idea Generation for
  Improved Performance

- The Lion's Way: How to Delegate and Empower Your Way to
  Success

- Better, Not Bitter: Using Coaching and Appraisals to Improve
  Performance

- Start Right, End Right: Successful Hiring and Safe Terminations

Find out more at www.professionalachievement.com

PROFIT
FROM THE
POWER OF MANY:
HOW TO USE MASTERMIND TEAMS
TO CREATE SUCCESS

Natalie D. Brecher

Professional Achievement Series®

Professional Achievement Series®

**Profit from the Power of Many:
How to Use Mastermind Teams to Create Success**

Copyright © MMIV Natalie D. Brecher

Find us on the Internet: www.professionalachievement.com

For sales inquiries, special prices for bulk quantities,
and for press review copies, author interviews, or other
publicity information, please contact the author,
Natalie D. Brecher, through: www.brecherassociates.com

Cover and Interior Design by Moxie & Magic, Ltd.
Photograph of the author: Copyright © MMIII Chris Campbell

ISBN: 0-9744990-0-5
Library of Congress Control Number: 2004100708

Printed in the United States

Is This Book for You?

This book is for you if you want to increase your professional achievements using the knowledge, skills, and talents of others; and at the same time, want to help those who help you.

If you are an entrepreneur or work in a small company, you will find forming a Mastermind Alliance of particular value—creating easy access to a team of knowledgeable people normally found only in large corporations.

Form a Mastermind Alliance to create a productive, effective, and rewarding team:

— on your own, to advance professional and/or personal achievements by creating a Personal Advisory and Support Board.

— within your company, to achieve business goals.

— within an association, to further committee goals.

— with other entrepreneurs to help develop and support your own business.

Table of Contents

Acknowledgments

- To the Wizards, for their support and collaborative efforts in our Mastermind Alliance
- To my lead cheerleader, Lyn Weiland, for her unwavering encouragement
- To my cheering section: Crystal Quimby, Chris Campbell, and Sandy Marrs
- To the numerous colleagues and friends who helped in this endeavor in many ways
- And to my husband, Tom Rasmussen, my finest Alliance

Introduction

Until I actually participated in a formal, on-going Mastermind Alliance, I thought I had benefited from the power of groups. Many times in my career, I have met with business associates or friends to discuss professional goals, search for solutions to business challenges, and the like, and usually found them to be helpful. In corporate environments, I enjoyed the benefits of teamwork, although primarily geared more to the organization's success versus the individual's success. While those experiences were positive, they were no measure of the power of a Mastermind Alliance.

When I joined my first Mastermind Alliance with a specific purpose in which all members shared a common goal, it was quite a revelation. One might think the formality of a structured group would limit innovation, promote political behavior, and serve no one with any individualized significant benefits. However, quite the reverse is true.

Just as a president has advisors to provide expertise in myriad areas, just as an athlete has fans to cheer her on, and just as a race car driver has a pit crew to keep him in the race, you too can have those resources with a Mastermind Alliance that is created and maintained properly.

There is power in working together. The Japanese expression, "Kyouzon, Kyouei" sums up a Mastermind: Exist and cooperate together, and prosper together.

The saying, "I may be one, but I am not alone," takes on new meaning when you are involved in a Mastermind Alliance. Whether directly or indirectly, you will receive knowledge, ideas, energy, and inspiration to result in a more powerful you. This not only helps you accomplish your goals, in addition, it allows you to do so with less effort and with more satisfaction as well.

An added benefit—a substantial one—is the ultimate rewards you will receive from helping your group members. A member has an issue to which you can bring a different perspective that results in a solution. Another member is finding it difficult to stay focused and motivated, and you provide guidance and support. The gifts you give to your group members are invaluable and an unending source of satisfaction to you as well.

In giving to others, in helping others achieve their goals, you are simultaneously creating a stronger, better you.

Do you want to benefit from the power of many? Create a Mastermind Alliance and you will.

Defining the Mastermind Concept

What is a Mastermind Alliance?

*"When a group of individual brains are
coordinated and function in harmony,
the increased energy created through
that alliance becomes available to every
individual brain in that group."*
~ Napoleon Hill

Although in its most rudimentary form, a Mastermind Alliance is a team working together, when properly created and maintained, it is also much more. It is using other people's knowledge, skills, and abilities as if they were your own.

A Mastermind Alliance is a "meeting of minds" in which participants put their knowledge, ideas, and experiences together to create a synergy and compilation of thoughts that benefits each member. It is a powerful method for stimulating dialog and the sharing of ideas to promote individual and collective achievements. Many successful people attribute their achievements to "masterminding."

Although Napoleon Hill is credited with bringing Mastermind Alliances to the public, the concept has been practiced for some time. Benjamin Franklin was a member of a Mastermind Alliance, which he called a Junto, that met weekly for many years. In his autobiography, he stated, "I had formed most of my ingenious acquaintances into a club for mutual improvement. Our club, the Junto, was found so useful and afforded such satisfaction to the members, that several were desirous of introducing their friends."

In his book, *Think and Grow Rich*, Napoleon Hill credited the "alliance" concept to Andrew Carnegie, industrialist, philanthropist, and founder of a highly successful steel corporation, which helped form U.S. Steel. Carnegie surrounded himself with people from various backgrounds to help him succeed.

In addition, Hill performed more than 20 years of research and analyzed the success of 500 people. As a result, he determined that having a Mastermind association was a critical element in the achievements of successful people. He believed that a group of like-minded, achievement-oriented individuals could dramatically leverage each other's success.

Hill defined "Master Mind" as:
> *"Coordination of knowledge and effort, in a spirit of harmony, between two or more people, for the attainment of a definite purpose. No individual may have great power without availing himself of the 'Master Mind.' Great power can be accumulated through no other principle!"*

The Mastermind concept has been proven beneficial many times over. Successful people report that the people with whom you associate are critical to your success. Walt Disney said, "Many hands, hearts, and minds generally contribute to anyone's notable achievements."

Stephen Covey, as Habit 6 in his book, *The 7 Habits of Highly Effective People*, recommends people "synergize." He says, "This is the habit of creative cooperation or teamwork. Synergy results from valuing differences by bringing different perspectives together in the spirit of mutual respect."

Robert G. Allen, author of *Creating Wealth*, and Mark Victor Hansen, coauthor of *Chicken Soup for the Soul*, call this type of alliance a "Dream Team" in their book, *The One Minute Millionaire*. They explain, "Associating with like-minded, success-oriented, joyful individuals—a Dream Team—is one of the most amazing success tools that exists. Anyone who achieves great success—anyone—must have a Dream Team."

A great deal has been said about the benefits of "partnering" and "strategic alliances" for businesses. Organizations know their strength is in numbers—the power of many.

Organizations such as Weight Watchers and Toastmasters operate on the premise that synergy is created through supportive groups. These types of groups result in greater individual accomplishments than when individuals work on their own. You may also find Mastermind groups in other forms such as The Executive Committee (TEC), CEO Roundtables, or Advisory Boards for private companies.

The popularity of using coaches to advance professional and personal accomplishments is increasing every day because of the exceptional benefits people derive from coaching. A Mastermind team creates a shared coaching environment so all members benefit.

The power of many greatly enhances the potential for achievement of an individual. In addition, the cumulative efforts of the group create an energy that fuels success. People benefit from the intelligence, experience, and support of others.

In its essence, a Mastermind Alliance is people helping people achieve a common purpose and their individual goals.

Organization Specific Application: In Businesses and Associations

"...the power of the team is so great that it is often wise to violate apparent common sense and force a team structure on almost everything."
~ Tom Peters

Businesses and associations are using the power of groups more often and more consistently. The group may be called a task force, committee, Quality Circle, or simply a team. Regardless of the label, Mastermind concepts and guidelines are applicable and can be used to create a group that is more effective and productive to the organization while resulting in more rewards to the individual team members.

Normally, a task force or committee is created in business by informing individuals they will be in the group; in associations, the group is formed by asking for volunteers. The group's purpose is stated, along with instructions and restrictions, such as a deadline, budget amount, or bylaws. After this initial formation, the group is left to its own devises to succeed or fail. Should a person within the group be experienced in creating effective groups, the group has a chance of succeeding. Without such expertise, if success comes, it will not come easily, and results may not be as beneficial as possible. Using the Mastermind Alliance concepts, a group has focus, direction, and a road map to ensure continued motivation, commitment, and success. Convert your team, task force, or committee into the power of a Mastermind Alliance.

Teams in Organizations (Businesses and Associations)	Mastermind Alliances
■ Typically authoritative	■ Participatory
■ Typically hierarchical	■ Equality
■ One purpose with individual members' purposes not recognized.	■ One common purpose with individual members' purposes recognized.
■ Leader is responsible for conduct and results.	■ All members are responsible for conduct and results.
■ Formatted structure	■ Formatted structure
■ Associations often use Robert's Rules of Order. Businesses normally use levels of command.	■ Mastermind Alliances use mutual respect and cooperative teamwork.

Special Note: In this book, at the end of each step to create and maintain a Mastermind Alliance, there is information regarding the application of the concepts specific to organizations that desire to improve the effectiveness and productiveness of their teams.

For your easy reference, these are entitled "Organization Specific Application" and will be found in gray boxes.

The Benefits of Mastermind Alliances

"I've learned one important thing about living. I can do anything I think I can—but I can't do anything alone. No one can go it alone. Create your team!"
~ Dr. Robert Schuller

A Mastermind Alliance helps its members achieve professional and/or personal goals in addition to the group's common purpose, by combining the sum total of the group's experience, education, talents, and innovative thoughts. The group becomes a source of inspiration, motivation, and energy; it provides ideas, support, and third-party viewpoints. Mastermind Alliances assist in solving problems, promoting innovation, and providing encouragement and support for achieving your personal and professional goals. Members improve their knowledge and skills as well as grow personally when exposed to the collective wisdom of a Mastermind Alliance. There is no better way to learn than from the collective knowledge of others.

In addition to the broad knowledge gained from the group members, the accountability factor can be a powerful motivator when applied in a supportive environment. Once a member commits to taking action on a goal, the other members hold him accountable. In a successful Mastermind Alliance, this does not result in the negative thinking of "having to report to the group." To the contrary, the member is motivated with the positive thinking of "wanting to please the members and make them proud." In a true Mastermind Alliance, when one member succeeds, every member succeeds.

It is difficult at times to stimulate your energy and maintain motivation, either when working alone or among unmotivated or negative people. A negative environment tends to drain your energy and damage your morale. When working with people enthusiastic about your efforts, who support and encourage you to reach your goals—as in a Mastermind Alliance—your achievements come more readily and more joyfully.

Enthusiasm and positive attitudes are contagious. When a member shares his or her enthusiasm and positive attitude, all members benefit. A Mastermind Alliance is a powerful source of energy and motivation.

In *Napoleon Hill's Keys to Success: The 17 Principles of Personal Achievement*, Hill describes the benefits of a Mastermind Alliance as:

> *"...intensifies your concentration... increases your faith, self-reliance, imagination, creative vision, personal initiative, enthusiasm, and will to win. You will keep moving toward your definite major purpose when you are surrounded by others who lend aid and encouragement..."*

Master Certified Coach, Teresia LaRocque, founder and CEO of TLC Teresia LaRocque Coaching and Associates in Vancouver, British Columbia, Canada, works with professionals, executives, and entrepreneurs in achieving their professional and personal goals. She highly recommends being part of a Mastermind.

"The spirit of collaboration, support, and accountability from a Mastermind group can be a crucial element of your success," LaRocque says. "The benefits of involvement are many, such as gaining clarity in your goals, determining the steps you should take to reach them, and the support that comes from other members."

LaRocque knows firsthand the benefits of a Mastermind Alliance, having been involved in two such groups. Her current group was formed two years ago with eight other coaches for the purpose of growing their businesses. She first learned of the Mastermind concept through Napoleon Hill's *Think and Grow Rich* book, and her work as a coach and trainer for Anthony Robbins and Associates.

"The greatest benefit I've received personally," she said, "is the energy I receive from my involvement and the feeling of having a safety net—knowing there are eight people in my corner helping me stretch out of my comfort zone."

Regardless of your exact goals and where you stand today on achieving them, a well-formed, effective Mastermind Alliance will benefit *you*...and other members as well. With the power of others, you will achieve more than you could possibly achieve on your own.

How Members Use a Mastermind Alliance

With their individual goals in mind, members tap into the knowledge of other members and use them as a sounding board. They ask for ideas on how to solve problems; they request honest (yet still supportive) feedback on action steps and any other issue imaginable.

Interviewing for a new job? Use your group to review your resume or role-play the interviewing process. Asking for a promotion or raise? Looking to generate more business? Want help solving business problems? Dealing with an employee and do not know how to handle him? Considering a new product or service to incorporate into your business?

You get the idea—the Mastermind Alliance is a resource for any challenge you wish to overcome or goal you wish to achieve. It will provide you with the ideas and momentum to achieve higher levels of success.

Creating a Mastermind Alliance

Step 1

Determine the Group's Purpose

*"Fix your eyes on perfection and you
make almost everything
speed towards it."
~ W.E. Channing*

There are two phases involved when determining the purpose of your Mastermind Alliance.

Phase One
Before you approach potential members, you must have a general purpose in mind so that concept and goal can be relayed to assess interest and compatibility.

Phase Two
After all members have committed, the group then clarifies the specific purpose the Mastermind Alliance will serve.

Phase One: Before You Approach Potential Members
As Stephen Covey advises, "Begin with the end in mind." That means before you approach potential members for the group, ask yourself what purpose the group will serve. There are myriad reasons Mastermind Alliances are formed. Typical

purposes might include: achieving professional goals, improving career success, changing careers, increasing business, or even forming a new business—or any combination of reasons.

Once you have a general purpose in mind, you are better equipped to know who to approach for inclusion in the group. The group's definitive purpose is decided once the Mastermind Alliance is formed.

In addition, you may consider how long you want the group to last. While some groups continue their association for many years, not all groups are intended to be long-term. Charles M. Bloom, Registered Principal, Registered Investment Advisor, and founder of Shoreline Wealth & Investment Management in Santa Barbara, California, participated in a Mastermind Alliance one hour per week for six months.

"Our purpose," he said, "was to share ideas and have discussions with people from different professions to offer unique perspectives."

Even with the group's short tenure, he reports the benefits were numerous. "The biggest benefit was learning to see issues from a different perspective. My achievements were more personal than professional—learning to be less judgmental and willing to see issues from perspectives other than mine, even if I ultimately went with my original preference," he said.

Bloom's short-lived Mastermind Alliance was a positive experience for him and the other members, and he recommends others get involved with a group as well. Asked why, he responded, "The opportunity to share and learn from others with different viewpoints and experiences is enriching and rewarding."

Considerations for Your Mastermind Alliance

■ What purpose do you want the group to serve?

■ Would that purpose serve others as well?

■ What benefits do you want to receive from participating?

■ Are there others you know who might desire the same benefits? In what other ways will members benefit?

■ Do you see the group as a long-term Mastermind Alliance or a temporary alliance to achieve short-term goals?

■ What characteristics do you want the group members to have?

■ Think of several people who stimulate your thinking, ignite your energy, and maintain your motivation. How do they help you?

■ Think of several people whose opinion you value because of their knowledge, experience, or other talents. How do they help you?

■ What do you have to offer the group?

■ What do you give back to people who seek your viewpoint?

■ How often do you want the group to meet?
Will those people you are considering
have time to commit fully?

Phase Two: After Members Have Been Chosen
Once you select your members (see Step 2), start your
group's first meeting with a discussion of the Mastermind
Alliance's purpose. It is vital to the group's success to determine a specific, clear, purpose to which every member will
lend support. What does each person want to accomplish?
What role do they want other members to play? What do
they expect from the group? How can they help each other?
Then use these responses to compose a short statement that
describes the purpose of the Mastermind Alliance. Use this
statement of purpose to set your meeting agenda, direct your
actions, and focus your thinking.

While members may define a purpose specific to your
group, all Mastermind Alliances share the principal purpose
that the participants work together to provide support and
assistance to everyone in achieving their individual goals.
Having supportive people whom you respect and who will
hold you accountable for achieving your goals is a powerful
motivator.

Review the group's overall purpose yearly. To do so,
answer these questions:

1. Is the Mastermind Alliance fulfilling its purpose?

2. Does the purpose still serve every member?

3. Do revisions need to be made?

Potential Applications for a Mastermind Alliance

There are numerous purposes a Mastermind Alliance can serve—professional and personal—limited only by one's imagination. Here are just a few.

- Sharing business "best practices"
- Business development
- Research and development
- New product or service ideas
- Performance improvement assessments and plans
- Problem-solving
- General brainstorming of business issues or evaluation of ideas
- Marketing and sales ideas
- Career growth/career planning
- Career change
- Study groups
- Volunteer committees
- Personal issues: financial goals (such as an Investment Club), raising children, health issues, etc.

Many people participate in more than one Mastermind Alliance.

Purposes within the Purpose

Within the Mastermind Alliance purpose, each member will have specific individual goals that closely align with the group's purpose. Members will also have specific benefits they wish to receive from the group. Each member should share with the group his specific purpose and desired benefits so the other members can be of greater assistance.

For example, if the purpose of the Mastermind Alliance is to improve career success, each individual will have a vision of what career success is to him or her. That vision will guide the action steps required to reach career success. The benefits a member may wish to receive could be: learning to network successfully, improving his writing skills, etc.

Organization Specific Application

Mastermind Alliances are extremely useful tools within organizations. An organization may elect to use a group of employees or volunteers for broad goals such as problem solving, research and development, idea generation, etc. Another use of groups is for specific tasks such as planning a conference, creating a marketing plan, or a special project of any purpose.

A few examples:

■ Form a group to streamline work processes in a particular department, such as accounting or production.

- Create a temporary Mastermind Alliance to address how to ensure an upcoming office move is efficient and easy on the employees.

- Form a group to research customers' (or employees') expectations of service and develop methods to improve the level of satisfaction.

- When formed for the purpose of performance improvement, there is no better method for finding solutions to problems and methods for improvement than to involve those who are closest to the situation and most affected by the issue.

- The concept of benchmarking (comparing your operations to other organizations and/or industries) results in many "Eureka!" discoveries. The power of such is greatly enhanced in a Mastermind Alliance. A group comprising people from different organizations with comparable business responsibilities can share "best practices" for learning and can work together on solving problems.

An essential (although unfortunately uncommon in organizations) approach to teamwork is to respect, address, and work to fulfill each member's purpose for being there—a strength of the Mastermind Alliance. While the team as an entity has a purpose, individual members have purposes too.

When a person voluntarily elects to be in a group, there is a direct motive and purpose for participating. When a member is part of the team because he or she was assigned, an indirect motivation and purpose is normally created by virtue of default. If the person feels as if he is a prisoner of the team, it is the team's goal to find a purpose(s) from which he can be motivated and gain benefits from his participation.

For example, the purpose could be to use the knowledge and/or skills the person enjoys using. The benefit could be to provide an opportunity for the member to learn something he would like to learn.

A Mastermind Alliance identifies a purpose that motivates each member and works to serve that purpose, along with achieving the goals of the group.

When the group is first formed, have each person communicate how she can best serve the group's purpose (the specific knowledge, skills, or abilities the person brings to the experience), and what she would like to gain from the team's work (how she can benefit from, or enjoy, the work). Even a member "assigned" by a supervisor can benefit from the group work...when a group takes the time to discover how each member can benefit.

Step 2

Select Members

*"There are very few Einsteins among us.
Most brilliance arises from ordinary
people working together in
extraordinary ways."
~ Roger Von Oech*

Proper selection of group members is critical to success and perhaps the most difficult component of creating an effective Mastermind Alliance. The choice should not be based on friendship, nor should it be based on business position. The overriding criteria for inclusion are the individual's ability to bring significant knowledge and the willingness to share that knowledge with others.

Your objective is not to create teacher-student or master-apprentice relationships in the group. Your objective is to create an evenly balanced group where every member can teach and every member can learn.

Select people who can help each other attain their goals in a team environment. These could be people in similar businesses and/or comparable levels of responsibilities in dissimilar businesses. Diversity in expertise and opinion will be a healthy component and helps bring varied perspectives to the group. Too much diversity (such as varied experience levels) may not be compatible with the other members or of value to them. If that is true, some members will not benefit as much from the Mastermind Alliance as do others.

An example of selecting members for a common purpose, yet with unique contributions, is the Wizards Mastermind group. Its purpose is to help members promote and operate their businesses. All members are consultants in assorted fields. They share a common type of work; however, members are not in competition with each other because each has a different type of client base.

Each member has strengths in areas other members do not. One member is extremely skillful at networking, one is savvy in marketing, one is knowledgeable about sales, etc. These various skill proficiencies allow the participants to develop in ways they would not grow without each other and allow each member to benefit from additional skills.

Another example of selecting members is a group formed to promote individual career success. Each member is employed by a different organization (two in the same business field, the others in various fields). One is an accountant, one is a retail manager, another is a computer programmer, etc. While they all share the goal of succeeding in their careers (as each personally defines), their different skills and perspectives help other members solve problems at work, consider how to advance their careers, provide support, and hold each other accountable for their career goals.

Once formed, adding a new member may only be accomplished with the unanimous vote of all members after careful evaluation. Consideration should be made for the interests of existing members, and the group must determine if the potential new member will work well within the group.

A new member under consideration should commit to attend a minimum of two meetings, and then the members evaluate and vote for (or against) inclusion.

Number

Although as few as two people may form a group and derive benefits, Mastermind Alliances work most effectively with five to eight members. This number will provide sufficient varied perspectives and ideas, yet allows each member to receive significant attention. In addition, too small a group may be less effective when some members cannot attend a meeting and does not provide a variety of input. In addition, too large a group can dilute individual benefits.

Qualities

All members should be people you trust and respect and whose opinions you value. Members should not be people who agree just to agree, nor should they be people who argue just to argue. An environment of growth will challenge all members in a positive, supportive manner.

While not an all-inclusive list, what follows are some of the qualities to look for in members to promote an effective Mastermind Alliance. Review this list and add other qualities you want in your group.

1. **A Giving Nature and the Willingness to Share**

   Perhaps the most important quality each member must have is the willingness to give more than he or she receives (both personally and professionally). Each member must benefit from the group or he will not remain a member. Each member must help other members reach their goals or it is not a true Mastermind Alliance.

2. Something to Give and the Time to Give It

Contributions from the group can come in the form of experience, education, innovative thinking, positive attitude, energy, and good judgment...any and all characteristics that help members achieve their goals. Each member must commit time to attend the meetings, execute his or her plans, and follow-through on those tasks that help other members as well.

3. Trustworthy

Integrity is paramount to the success of the group. Each member must treat all information as confidential to cultivate trust and confidence, leaving what is said in the meeting room.

4. Works in Harmony with Others

The Mastermind Alliance is for the benefit of every member individually and the group as an entity. Every member must not only want to win, in addition, he must want to win for others as well. Consider how every decision affects other members. While each member will have his personal goals, hidden intents and goals can hinder, if not destroy, the group's effectiveness.

5. Shared Values and Ethics

Every person has her own concept of what is important and what is acceptable behavior. A meshing of these beliefs among group members makes for a more productive, positive environment.

6. Alert to Other Members' Needs and Active

Being a good listener and being empathetic to people's needs are essential elements that help other members achieve their goals. Members should actively participate in discussions and activities.

7. Looks at Solutions and Does Not Dwell on Problems

Some people are more prone to dwell on problems, and a group can provide an audience for such. All members should be those who can concisely state the problem and then concentrate their individual efforts on finding solutions. This is for every member's benefit.

8. Offers Support and Productive Criticism

Support each member's efforts in achieving his or her goals in an understanding, caring manner. The purpose of a group member is not to criticize, but to provide support and generate ideas that will benefit individuals and the group. However, when criticism of a member's ideas or plan seems warranted, it must be done in a productive manner. (See "How to Handle Potential Pitfalls" in Step 8.)

Types of Members

*"No one can be the best at everything.
But when all of us combine our talents,
we can be the best at virtually anything."*
~ Don Ward

Members may be found in many places. Consider the following sources to determine the people to include in your Mastermind Alliance. The benefits of having a variety of "types" are to have a variety of expertise, diverse points of view, and develop an environment of creative thought.

Coworkers
People with whom you work can have much in common with each other and share common goals. However, be careful with this choice, as you do not want your group to be a duplication of what happens at work.

Business Associates
Mentors and role models: people in your field or with whom you do business. Many groups maintain a standard that members may not be in direct business competition with each other; however, this does not mean you cannot be in the same field of work.

Outside Experts
People in different fields of work from your own whose success, achievements, and professional behavior could add value to the group members.

Guest Speakers/Participants
Consider including people outside the group when specific knowledge/input normally not available among members would be of benefit. People are often very agreeable to share their expertise with an appreciative group.

Organization Specific Application

Membership positions may be filled with employees/volunteers from within the company/association, as is most common. However, seriously consider including people from different organizations—whether within your industry or outside. This is especially effective when issues are new to the organization; conflict resides within the organization; new perspectives are critical for success; and for the purpose of benchmarking.

Businesses can also benefit from mixing employees of diverse disciplines; i.e., people with various knowledge and skills. For example, a customer service-oriented Mastermind Alliance could include representatives from accounting, engineering, and marketing. These assorted perspectives can add a unique vision and varied thinking to the group.

Dr. W. Edwards Deming, internationally renowned consultant whose work revolutionized Japanese industry, addresses teamwork in one of his 14 Points that encapsulates his philosophy:

"Break down barriers between departments. People in research, design, sales, and production must work as a team, to foresee problems of production and in use that may be encountered with the product or service."

Step 3

Choose the Form of Leadership/Facilitation

"The coach is the team,
and the team is the coach.
You reflect each other. "
~ Sparky Anderson

As with any type meeting, it is best to use a leader/facilitator to keep the group members focusing, following the agenda, and supporting the Mastermind Alliance purpose. While decisions (such as meeting dates and format) should be made by consensus or vote, the group needs a leader to ensure meetings are focused and decisions are carried out.

Duties, however, are not restricted to the chairperson/facilitator. In addition to the responsibilities of serving as a member (See Step 8, "Maintaining a Mastermind Alliance"), there are other positions you may elect to assign. All positions contribute to the effectiveness of your meetings.

A Mastermind Alliance need not be an entity following the formal structure of Robert's Rules of Order with motions and such; indeed, such formality may inhibit the free-flowing exchange of ideas and support. Nonetheless, some formality and duties must be maintained for the group to be efficient and effective.

Chairperson/Facilitator

This position ensures the agenda is followed and sees that every member has the opportunity to speak and gain benefits from the meeting. Involving all group members starts when developing the agenda and flows throughout the meeting. The chairperson/facilitator:

- Controls the meeting process.
- Keeps participants following and focusing on the agenda.
- Encourages participation from all members, including those with opinions in the minority.
- Elicits feedback.
- Prompts questions.
- Requests clarification of vague statements.
- Advances consensus when consensus is required.
- Ends the meeting by providing a brief summary of action items and decisions.

This requires a strong stance at times to redirect the members and enforce the agenda. The chairperson/facilitator must be able to confront and hold people accountable. Many groups rotate the chairperson on occasion (some groups rotate for each meeting), allowing each member the opportunity to act as chairperson.

The chairperson/facilitator must balance his or her role with that of a participant. This can be a daunting task. However, a Mastermind Alliance is for the benefit of all members: all members are equal. The difficulty inherent in this balancing act supports the concept of rotating the position.

Coordinator

The coordinator will set meeting dates that are scheduled to accommodate members' schedules and arrange for meeting sites, food, and so on. This position can also be rotated.

Some see this position as a small part in the Mastermind Alliance; however, it is actually a very important role. Setting mutual meeting dates alone can be a difficult task at best.

Timekeeper

It can be difficult to uphold a meeting agenda's timing, even for the most focused. Using a clock or timer, the timekeeper notifies the group when it is time to move on in the agenda. The timekeeper ensures the meeting starts on time, the agenda items are followed, and the meeting stops as scheduled.

Rather than have the chairperson/facilitator act as the timekeeper to follow the agenda, this task may be assigned to another member. Having the task assigned to a designated person can eliminate the "we have run out of time" predicament.

Secretary/Recorder

A secretary/recorder should be assigned should you choose to keep minutes or maintain a record of the goals and projects of each member. This is not a requirement; however, it does assist in monitoring progress. As with other positions, the secretary's duties may be rotated as well.

Notes should be concise and not serve as a transcript of the meeting. At minimum, the secretary/recorder should maintain a record with a general overview of the meeting (this can be the agenda); the decisions and action items to which the members have committed; and the plans for the next meeting. A sample format follows.

Meeting Record
—Sample—

Date _____

Time _____

Place _____

In Attendance
List the names of those attending the meeting.

General Overview
Provide a brief narrative summary. Attach the agenda and any supporting documents.

Decisions/Action Items	**Who**	**When**
Description	*Name*	*Date Due*
For example:		
1. Write magazine article	Tom	5 May
2. Approach XYZ Company for partnership	Stacey	19 May
3. Create a marketing plan	Wendy	18 June

Open Items for Future Discussion
List unresolved topics/issues and those to include in future meetings, with agenda date if applicable.

Next Meeting

Date _____

Time _____

Place _____

Organization Specific Application

It is stereotypical practice that an organization dictates "who is in charge" of any team it creates. With committees, a chairperson is elected; in companies, the senior level employee is normally the leader. However, what if that was not the case? What if the chairperson/facilitator role was given to a junior employee? What if the highest-level executive served in the role of the secretary/recorder? How would that affect the group?

What if the roles were rotated? Rotating positions disturbs the usual politics of the hierarchy. (Yes, every team has a hierarchy, and changing it can create different results.) Would commitment to the purpose be enhanced? Can accountability be increased with deeper participation?

For groups to be effective, every member must feel that he or she has the ability to contribute and that those contributions will be considered as equally as the contributions of other members. By changing the status quo from one leader with members who implement tasks, to all members being equal (as with the Mastermind concept), the results of the group's work can exceed expectations.

Step 4

Establish Values: Standards of Behavior

*"When people honor each other, there is
a trust established that leads to synergy,
interdependence, and deep respect. Both
parties make decisions and choices
based on what is right, what is best,
what is valued most highly."*
~ Blaine Lee

The group must create an atmosphere that sustains the purpose of the Mastermind Alliance in addition to advancing the growth of each member and the attainment of individual goals, while providing each other support and trust.

The group should create a list of guidelines describing values—how members will behave. Some examples for consideration:

1. **Commitment to attend meetings and arrive on time**
   What happens if members consistently miss meetings? How will late arrivals be handled?

2. *Confidentiality*
   The Mastermind Alliance must provide a confidential forum for all discussions. Depending on the profile of the members, there may be potential for competition, which makes confidentiality crucial. Will there be penalties if confidentiality is not honored?

3. *Participation to advance the accomplishments of members*
   The adage "one for all and all for one" is the foundation of teamwork, and a Mastermind Alliance is a team. When the underlying current of your group is to help others succeed in their goals, your group will be a success. Receiving help is inspired by giving help: This requires members have a giving nature and a strong sense of self.

4. *Commitment to setting and making progress toward individual goals*
   If a member does not set her specific goals or makes no progress in achieving her goals, can the member continue to participate?

5. *Accountability*
   Being held accountable for making progress toward goals is a strong motivating force in a Mastermind Alliance. Members must agree to hold each other accountable. If a member does not follow through on his or her plans, other mem-

bers are obliged to hold the member accountable—in a respectful manner.

6. *Maintain a supportive environment*
A positive attitude and encouragement can overcome the worst of times and propel people to success. Cheer your members, congratulate them on small achievements, and celebrate accomplishments.

7. *Bring solutions, not problems; be a problem solver, not a problem enabler*
Misery loves company, and it is far too easy to fall into the trap of complaining about difficulties rather than seek answers to challenges. Every member must focus on solutions, for that is a purpose and benefit of a Mastermind Alliance.

8. *Respect others*
In a group setting, respect comes in many forms. It manifests itself in active listening without judgment; in providing feedback in a supportive manner; in providing constructive criticism; in allowing people to be true to their nature—not attempting to make them more to your liking; and in placing value in the opinions that differ from yours. Treat others as they want to be treated...in doing so you will earn their respect as well.

9. *Share time*
Unlike many corporate or board of directors' meetings, in a Mastermind Alliance

meeting it is extremely crucial that all members receive equal attention in both the ability to speak and the ability to be heard.

10. Accept a member's right to reticence on occasion
There may be times a member chooses not to participate as much as other times—this must be respected just as the right to participate must be respected.

A Mastermind group that has been together for one year experienced one of its members attending fewer and fewer meetings. When asked if he wanted to remain in the Mastermind Alliance, he enthusiastically said yes; however, he still failed to participate in meetings or in e-mail messages the group members sent.

The group had to decide: Do they unilaterally remove him or allow his behavior to continue? In response, they created a set of values/behaviors for the members to follow, which they called Codes of Conduct. One of these codes required that attendance at the meetings be a minimum of 75 percent.

This requirement was then relayed to the nonparticipating member and asked if he would agree to comply. Although he stated his desire to remain in the group, he also said he could not comply with the attendance requirement because of his busy schedule. The final result? An underperforming member was removed without conflict because required behaviors were set.

Organization Specific Application

Typically overlooked in companies and associations, agreeing on and setting standards for behavior builds a foundation for a team's success. When values are discussed and determined by consensus, the chances of all members' behaviors supporting the group's efforts are increased. Should a member disagree with the group's values, it is crucial to the success of the group to remove that member.

A business that implemented Mastermind concepts into a project team reported improved results by merely agreeing on behaviors to which each member would adhere and asking how each member could benefit from his or her working on the project.

The team had been working together during weekly meetings for several months with no visible progress reaching its goal. The team leader found the members were not working together cohesively, nor making the team's project a priority because of the daily demands on their time.

He gathered the team and asked that they determine how the group should work together to achieve its goal and in what way members could be rewarded for their efforts.

The group created a list of ten behaviors and the reward they wanted. Expecting individual rewards, the supervisor was surprised to find the reward was team-based. The group decided that the reward would be based not only on achieving the project's goals; in addition, to receive the reward, each member must have adhered to the agreed-upon behaviors. The members decided that, should a member not work within the behaviors, he or she could not participate in the reward.

The reward? A simple celebration at a special restaurant. The supervisor wholeheartedly agreed, and the project was completed successfully.

Step 5

Create a Name

*"Enthusiasm is the mother of effort,
and without it nothing great
was ever achieved."*
~ Ralph Waldo Emerson

Creating a name is not a requirement; however, doing so helps establish an identity. By generating excitement and loyalty, it creates a sense of team.

For example, one Mastermind group calls itself the "Wizards of Genius"; another group calls itself "The Royal Order." What name excites your members?

Some Mastermind Alliances create a logo for the group to create even more excitement, adding it to notebooks, signs...even baseball caps. Maybe your group will have an anthem!

A sports team knows the power of its name—creating enthusiasm and eliciting loyalty. Its colors, logo, and even its mascot bring a sense of unity and excitement to the athletes and the fans. Use that same power for your Mastermind Alliance.

Organization Specific Application

Esprit de corps is essential for teams to operate successfully. In business environments, when pressures can be intense, what better way to lighten the pressure and create a sense of unity? The mere reference to being a member of a Mastermind Alliance, versus a task force, may bring an improved perspective on the assignment.

For example, create a name for the marketing Mastermind group: The Marketing Marvels. Create a name for the newsletter committee: The News Hounds. Have a little fun with a name to create excitement, unity, and loyalty.

Step 6

Schedule Meetings

*"A hurricane:
many individual raindrops cooperating."*
~ Unknown

Once the first five steps are completed, it is time to schedule Mastermind Alliance meetings, which will fit with the members' schedules.

Where

Face-to-face meetings are best and can be held just about anywhere space permits: an office, someone's home, a meeting room, a local community center, a library, even a park. Some groups elect to meet at restaurants, however, make certain the area is conducive to an effective meeting without interruptions. When it is not possible to meet personally, "immediate messaging" on the Internet, Web-cast meetings, or conference calls can be used.

When and How Long

There are many time schedules for meetings that can work for Mastermind groups. Any frequency can be scheduled as long as it is acceptable and beneficial to your members. These can be morning, afternoon—even evening meetings.

Examples include:

- Many Mastermind Alliances meet once a month for at least three hours, depending on the meeting content for that session and the number of members.
- Other groups meet once a week or twice a month.
- Some groups have a short monthly meeting and add longer meetings (half- or full-day) quarterly, semi-annually, or annually.
- Still other groups successfully meet only four times each year, however, those meetings are normally one to two days in length.

Any and all scenarios are plausible. Choose the format that makes sense for your purpose and your members' needs. Allow your group members to determine the frequency and time as desired and needed. Set up a regular schedule for meetings (e.g., the first Thursday of every month) and adhere to time frames: start on time and stay focused on the agenda.

Attendance at every meeting should be mandatory, unless an emergency or critical commitment indicates otherwise. An attending member should report the essence of the meeting to any members not in attendance.

Frequent Contact

To keep the momentum going and create a strong team, members should communicate individually between meetings to share information or serve the needs of other members. Stay in contact between regularly scheduled meetings with phone calls, letters, faxes, and e-mail messages.

Costs

Unlike many meetings, especially those held in hotels and other venues, Mastermind Alliance meetings are normally no- or low-cost meetings. The venue is normally "donated" by a member, and those wanting refreshments and/or food will most often simply divide the costs among those attending the meeting.

Some groups will assess dues after budgeting costs; however, this will require some accounting of the funds. Dues work best when there are substantial costs incurred on behalf of the Mastermind Alliance. For example, one group participated in joint advertising of its members' services on a regular basis, and the dues covered these costs.

Organization Specific Application

In business environments, the modus operandi for meetings is to schedule them within business hours and within the confines of the office. While this is certainly functional, consider holding special meetings before or after work hours, and in a setting away from the workplace...at least, on occasion. Often, employees are distracted from the group's work because, in their minds, their phones are still ringing, and the office environment reminds them of the work remaining on their desks. A new setting not only helps people focus, in addition, it can prompt varied perspectives and enhance creativity.

How Long

Too often, business and association meetings are squeezed in-between other commitments, which does not allow for the development of ideas and the thorough execution of plans. Depending on the status of the group's planning and level of progress, many times, more can be accomplished by meeting less often for longer periods-of-time.

For example, meeting one half-day per quarter, versus one hour per month, may produce better results with less effort. Longer meetings held less frequently could be less disruptive to daily business than short meetings held more frequently.

Prime examples are association committee meetings held monthly, and company departments holding the proverbial weekly meeting because "we have always done it this way." Discuss alternatives with the group members, and allow the purpose and needs of the group to determine when and how long meetings should be held.

Step 7

Determine the Meeting Agenda

*"Here is a basic rule
for winning success.
The rule is: success depends on the
support of other people.
The only hurdle between you
and what you want to be
is the support of others."*
~ David Joseph Schwartz

There are many ways to conduct a Mastermind meeting, and every group should follow an agenda that works for it. A group may structure the agenda so each member is given specific time to discuss her or his goals, progress towards those goals, and receive input from other members. Conversely, a meeting may be structured so the group concentrates on a common goal or question.

Written Agenda
A written agenda distributed prior to the meeting that includes topic(s) for discussion and time allocation serves to allow all members to prepare for the meeting and is essential to keep the group focused. If any documents will be used during the meeting, they should be distributed with the agenda.

Circulate the agenda and any addenda at least a week prior to the meeting—perhaps longer, depending on your group members' schedules and the length of preparation time required. This is an issue you want to discuss when first forming your Mastermind Alliance and set a standard for distribution of the agenda.

A major problem with meetings is that participants too often stray from the subject matter on the agenda or the issue being discussed. An agenda and timekeeper, along with a strong chairperson/facilitator can keep this under some control; however, all members must remain conscientious of the difficulty, and when finding the conversations off track, take measures to regain focus.

Master Certified Coach, Teresia LaRocque's Mastermind group reports their greatest challenge was that of initially not having enough structure during their weekly telephone conferences and at their quarterly retreats. The challenge was solved, however, by creating a format for their meetings and all members using discipline to adhere to the agenda.

"We felt we were leaving the meetings without a lot of progress. Our new format allows us a few minutes to check in and talk about how we're doing, and then we address anyone's burning issues for the week. At first, we thought everyone would participate and it would take more time; however, since we meet often, there are usually just a few major issues. To close, each member discusses his or her focus for the week. We've found this format really works for us."

Meeting Formats
Try not to be restricted to a certain agenda, however. There are times when the agenda should change. Try new ways and see what works best for your group. Here are some helpful tips:

1. Agree on a different focus issue for each meeting. This may be accomplished by consensus, vote, or by one member determining the focus issue for one meeting, another member selecting the issue for the next meeting, and so on until all members have contributed and then starting the process over again. Knowing the focus issue allows each member to be prepared to get the most from each meeting.

2. Especially as your group becomes closer, it is easy to get in the habit of spending too much time on socializing and/or storytelling. Socializing is an important aspect for the health of the group; however, time is always an issue for meetings. Some groups solve this by having a designated "social time" 15 minutes prior to, and/or 15 minutes after, the meeting.

3. An energizing way to start a meeting is for every member to share something positive he has accomplished or that has happened to him since the last meeting. This starts everything off on a positive note. One of the joys of a Mastermind Alliance is celebrating the "wins" as well as providing encouragement and support with challenges.

4. Each member provides an update, reporting what she is currently working on and areas where she needs support or input.

Your group may decide to have the member report, and then 1) each member provides feedback individually, or 2) members participate in an open forum of discussion. The member requesting input may be the one who designates how she would like the group to respond.

5. Each member brings something to contribute to the group. This could be a magazine article, a tape, a book, contact name, etc.

6. Spend 10-15 minutes with each member who wants the group's help. However, not every member may need the group's attention at every meeting.

An alternative is to devote a major portion of a meeting to one member, spending most of the group's time on that individual's needs. At the next meeting, work with another member, and so forth, until every member has had his turn. This works well only when you meet a minimum of once a month, as you do not want too much time to pass without addressing other members' needs.

Do not end your meetings inconclusively. A few minutes at the end to summarize and note action items and decisions will not only bring closure, in addition, it will serve as reinforcement of the meeting's benefits.

Sample Agendas

Three sample agendas for a six-member group are provided. Try these with your Mastermind Alliance, adjusting the timing according to the number of members you have, and try a different agenda as well. Find out what works best for your group and what works best given the situation at the time of each meeting.

Sample Agenda 1: For a Six-member Group

6 @ 10 minutes	1. Quick update by each member: a. Good news; something positive she has accomplished or experienced b. Share contributions (helpful information) with the group c. What has happened since the last meeting d. Report of how she is doing/did on meeting her goals e. What she is working on and how the group can help
30 minutes total	2. Focus issue of this meeting, discussed as a group
6 @ 10 minutes	3. Member specific time (time for each member): For input from other members on any issue(s) she would like to discuss.
6 @ 5 minutes	4. Close with each member reporting: a. Goals/challenges for future he wants to accomplish by the next meeting b. How other members can help or support
60 minutes	5. Adjourn for lunch to allow for socializing

Total: 4 Hours (3 hours of business time)

Sample Agenda 2: For a Six-member Group

10 minutes	1. Socialize
10 minutes	2. Each member reports a "win" (something positive he has accomplished or experienced)
15 minutes	3. Share contributions (helpful information) with the group
30 minutes	4. Discuss the focus issue (determined by the group at a previous meeting)
6 @ 15 minutes	5. Member specific time (for each member):
	a. What has happened since the last meeting
	b. What he has accomplished since the last meeting
	c. What he is working on
	d. What goals he would like to reach before the next meeting
	e. How the group can help him achieve those goals
10 minutes	6. Group determines the next meeting's focus issue
10 minutes	7. Open Forum
5 minutes	8. Socialize

Total: 3 Hours (2 hours, 45 minutes of business time)

Sample Agenda 3: For a Six-member Group

This sample uses the agenda in Sample 2, except the "member specific time" (number 5 below) is focused on only one individual in this scenario. A variation would be to allocate time to two to three members per meeting.

10 minutes	1. Socialize
10 minutes	2. Each member reports a "win" (something positive he has accomplished or experienced)
15 minutes	3. Share contributions (helpful information) with the group
30 minutes	4. Discuss the focus issue (determined by the group at a previous meeting)
1 @ 1 hour	5. Individual member specific time
	a. What has happened since the last meeting
	b. What he has accomplished toward since the last meeting
	c. What he is working on
	d. What goals he would like to reach before the next meeting
	e. How the group can help him achieve those goals

Alternatives to this include allocating 30 minutes to two members, or adding another hour to the meeting to give two members an hour each. The options are endless.

10 minutes	6. Group determines the next meeting's focus issue
40 minutes	7. Open Forum
5 minutes	8. Socialize

Total: 3 Hours (2 hours, 45 minutes of business time)

Organization Specific Application

The purpose of Mastermind groups in organizations will greatly determine the format of the meeting. Decide on formats and agendas by consensus to create more "ownership" in the outcome. In addition to working toward meeting the group's goals, address the individual member's purposes as well. Schedule time to discuss if each member is benefiting from the group in addition to whether the group is serving its purpose.

Maintaining a Mastermind Alliance

Step 8

Maintain Effectiveness and Productivity

*"Great discoveries and achievements
invariably involve the cooperation
of many minds."*
~ Alexander Graham Bell

Once your group is created, the work has just begun, and the benefits will depend on the efforts each member takes to make the group a success. To maintain a positive, effective Mastermind Alliance, it must be cultivated and nurtured as you would a garden. Work diligently and constantly to strengthen the harmony of the group and benefits to all members.

Each member must derive benefits or he or she will not remain in the group. It takes work to keep the group focused and valuable to all members. Confront problems early, constructively, and consistently.

Your efforts will be worthwhile...the power of many is now at your fingertips.

Organization Specific Application

Maintaining a business team or association committee as a Mastermind Alliance has a few distinctions:

- Unless it is strictly volunteer-based, most members will be assigned and therefore commitment to the purpose may not be as strong.

- Accustomed to "normal" team or committee work, members will be habituated to *not* having their individual purposes and/or desired benefits addressed.

- Business environments can stifle teamwork.

To counteract these differences so there is willing cooperation, it is imperative that the leader take certain steps to ensure the success of the team.

1. "Sell" the members on the purpose of the team. What is the vision? What are the benefits of success?

2. Inform members how the team and individual participation fits into the bigger picture of the organization and the importance of their role.

3. Subordinate the leader's role to the group's purpose. Rotating the chairperson/facilitator role can assist in that regard.

4. Members should be trained in participative management, problem-solving, and conflict resolution.

5. The individual needs of, and benefits for, the members must be a high priority in order to maintain motivation.

6. Members must receive rewards to remain committed to the group's purpose. Reward group results, not individual efforts.

> As W. Edwards Deming states in *Out of the Crisis*, "Good performance on a team helps the company but leads to less tangible results to count for the individual."

> Tom Peters, author of *Thriving on Chaos*, believes, "Rewards should go to teams as a whole. Evaluation, even for members who are only full-time for a while, should be based principally upon team performance."

Your Role as a Mastermind Member

*"The greatest good you can do for others
is not just to show your riches
but reveal to them their own."*
~ Benjamin Disraeli

Although a collective effort, the benefits each member receives will be in direct proportion to what he or she gives to the Mastermind Alliance. Each member is responsible for the success (or failure) of the group. Being an effective group member takes knowledge, skill, a supportive attitude, and the commitment to make the group a success. All members are equal regardless if serving as chairperson/facilitator, coordinator, or secretary/recorder. The process of the meetings, the content, and the manner in which the group functions are under the control of all members.

To add value to the group, prepare for every meeting-conduct research if needed. Consider what you can take to the meeting that will assist with a member's goals or the group's purpose.

Contribute to the Success of Others
Always remember that you are not in competition with your group members—you are in partnership. Your ability to contribute to the success of your colleagues is the major reason you are a member of the Mastermind Alliance. Contribute

freely and often, and do not seek an unfair advantage at the expense of others. When a member expresses a goal or action step, you should ask yourself, "What can the group and/or I do to assist this person in achieving his goals?"

Participate
When contributing to discussions, speak when your contribution is relevant. Should the conversation proceed to another topic, do not try to backtrack, which can disrupt the flow of the meeting. Instead, make a note of your thought, and revisit it during an open forum or at the close of the meeting.

Respect the Meeting Process
Consider the facilitator's role. If you believe the process is not going as planned, a member is not being recognized, or another issue is harming the group, it is your responsibility to act. Talk to the facilitator in private if you feel more comfortable doing so.

You may also provide discreet input during the meeting should the problem be one that can be handled straightforwardly. For example, saying, "John, I think you stopped Maggie from finishing her thought," may serve adequately to improve the situation.

Listen
When others speak, give them your full attention. Not only does it show respect, it will also allow you to benefit from the discussion. Do not hold side conversations; it will only serve to break the focus of the meeting.

Be Positive
Evaluating ideas before they have had a chance to mature is a common behavior. Look for value in what is being said; do not jump to conclusions or merely see the negative. If asked for input on an idea you feel is not valuable, first say what

you like about it, and then follow up with a concern-and-a possible solution.

Be Open to Criticism

Every member is a part of the Mastermind Alliance for the same purpose and to reach similar goals. The knowledge and ideas in the group will not always correspond with yours, thus there will be times your thoughts or actions will be criticized. Remember, you are there to benefit from other people's knowledge and ideas. Stay open to criticism and use it to grow. Try not to take it as a personal attack.

Assessing Problems

*"The significant problems we have
cannot be solved at the same level
of thinking with which
we created them."*
~ Albert Einstein

As with any group, it is easy (and predictable) to function in the same way every time you meet. While there is a great deal of good in consistency, it may also have a defeating effect if the way you are functioning is ineffective or if your group has begun behaving on autopilot and no creative thought or actions are being introduced.

At least twice a year, devote some time at your meeting to assess how your Mastermind Alliance is working. Some of the questions you will want to address are these: Is the purpose still accurate? How is the group fulfilling its purpose? How is the group helping all members? What can be done to improve?

A method for improvement can be taken from the process used in performance improvement assessments. To use those methods, look at your group as the center between forces that are sustaining it and forces that are restraining it. Identify processes and behaviors that are positive, which keep the group functioning effectively and providing benefits to all members. Then identify processes and behaviors that are negative, which prevent the group from being its best. Working collectively, make a list of those processes and behaviors. Afterward, discuss each one and determine how the Mastermind Alliance should continue (and possibly improve) the positives. Then address the negatives: How can they be eliminated or changed for the better?

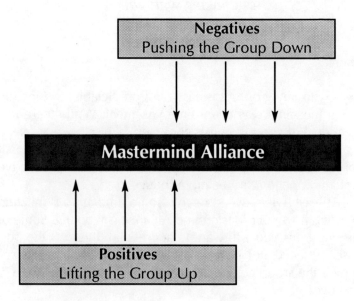

How to Handle Potential Pitfalls

*"He only profits from praise
who values criticism."
~ Heinrich Heine*

Group members must address potential problems resulting from members' behavior promptly by bringing the issue to the attention of the offending member. Watch for members who are:

- Not contributing as the others do (in quantity or quality).

- Not being supportive.

- Not working in harmony and not looking for win/win positions.

- Bringing problems and not solutions.

- Providing advice on every issue.

- Absorbing more of the group's resources (such as attention time) than other members do.

Nine Steps for Productive Criticism

Criticism, of course, is often difficult to accept. For best results, approach it in a tactful, sensitive manner. Here is a nine-step process to use when dealing with an under-performing group member to present criticism in a productive and effective light.

1. Before you begin, make sure your intent is to help; focus your attention on a "win-win" solution.

2. Meet with the person in private.

3. Explain the unacceptable behavior in simple, clear terms with specific examples. What is the problem—exactly? Being vague does not protect the person from hurt; it merely negates the effectiveness of the criticism and frustrates the recipient.

4. Describe the impact/effect of the behavior (how it affects the person, the group, and the company), so the person understands the consequences of his actions/behavior.

5. State the desired outcome and how the actions should change. Describe—in measurable terms—the acceptable behavior.

6. Describe the benefits of change for the individual, for the team, and for the company, so the person can see why he should change.

7. Encourage feedback by asking what the person thinks about what has been said. Make the conversation a two-way discussion.

8. Express the belief that she or he can change, and that you expect a positive result. Knowing someone supports you can go a long way to produce change.

9. Ask what he or she can do to change the behavior, and then jointly discuss and set a deadline for the action steps. Ask what the group, the company—and you—can do to support making the change.

To achieve maximum cooperation, conduct steps 3–7 and 9 as questions. For example, "What do you think about today's meeting? What could you do differently to be of more value to the group? How would you make those changes? What benefits do you think you will gain when these changes are made?"

Tips for Delivering Criticism

When providing constructive criticism, use these tips to express your thoughts to create a non-defensive atmosphere.

- Whenever possible, use questions so the under-performing team member can reflect on her behavior and consider the consequences of not changing, the manner in which she should behave, and the benefits of changing.
  For example:
  — How do you think you are contributing to the group?
  — How do you think missing so many meetings is affecting the group?

— If you act more supportive, how do you think the group members will respond?

■ The language used should not be global in nature: words such as "always" and "never." Saying, "You are *never* supportive," is probably not true. Instead, use a specific example, such as, "I felt you were non-supportive when you said Stacey could not achieve her goal."

■ Use "I" talk, not "you" talk. This means taking responsibility for the viewpoint you are expressing, e.g., "*I* feel Todd is not getting enough attention from the group," versus "*You* do not give Todd enough attention."

■ Use passive versus active voice. Instead of, "You gave advice to every problem today, "say, "It comes across as if you know the answer to every challenge when so much advice is given. Can you redirect your participation to help people come to their own conclusions versus giving an answer? We can all learn more using that technique."

■ Ask for their thoughts. If information is presented about an unknown point or perspective you have not considered, be willing to say you are wrong.

Personality Types

There are a several personality types that can hinder your group's effectiveness. Harmony and cooperation are paramount to the success of a Mastermind Alliance; therefore, poor performers, or those not adding value to the group, should be addressed straightaway.

Here are six personalities you may find in your group at one time or another that will stifle the group's effectiveness and how to resolve the challenges they create.

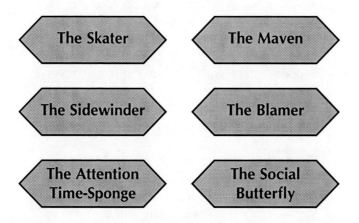

The Skater

The Maven

The Sidewinder

The Blamer

The Attention
Time-Sponge

The Social
Butterfly

The Skater

When faced with a team member who appears to be allowing others to do most of the work or not participating as much as others are, most people's instinct is to assume he is lazy or trying to get by with the minimum amount of work (or none at all). Do *not* make this assumption. Doing so can alienate a member who has a great deal to offer, however, for reasons other than laziness is not being of value to the Mastermind Alliance.

To resolve:
First, put the onus on the team itself. Consider how the group (the leader, members, structure, etc.) is affecting this person. What could be done to help him participate? Is he being asked to do things he cannot because of a lack of knowledge, skills, or abilities? Have any of his contributions been accepted by the group? What can he gain from the group? How is he being rewarded?

Second, meet with him and through questions (make no assumptions), ask him about his participation and if he feels he is getting any benefits from the Mastermind Alliance.

Third, use the "Nine Steps and Tips for Delivering Productive Criticism" (found in the "How to Handle Potential Pitfalls" section in Step 8) to counsel him on his behavior.

Fourth, should interventions with the member result in the viewpoint that the group

would be better without him—after every-thing has been tried to resolve the prob-lem—use questions to allow him to remove himself from the group. For example:
"How do you think we can resolve this so the group functions more productively?" For a more direct approach, you may ask, "Would you be happier if you were not involved with the group?"

The Maven (Know-it-All)
In a Mastermind Alliance, it can be easy to fall into the role of "advice giver," especially for those with more experience, education, or talent. While members can ask for advice, and in fact receive advice, each member must exercise caution and not attempt to be the mentor for all members. Members are not there to impose their opinions or hand out answers. When a maven shows himself, the chairperson or another member should see to it that other members have the chance to par-ticipate. A Mastermind Alliance is a team, and a team protects all its members.

Sample comments to address the issue: "We've not heard from Wendy and Bob yet; I'd like to hear their perspectives." Alternatively, "Perhaps we should go around the table, and receive comments from each member."

The Sidewinder
The sidewinder is the person who engages in conversations on the side of the main discus-

sion. While there is normally no destructive intent, it nevertheless disrupts the flow of the Mastermind purpose by distracting the members from the topic being discussed.

To resolve:
A nonverbal solution may be all that is needed: merely stop talking and resume the meeting when the conversation stops, which it will when silence overcomes the room. For a more direct approach, you may say, "I'm sorry, John, would you like to address the group?" Of course, if the behavior continues, you will have to ask pointedly for them to stop.

The Blamer
Although the Mastermind group's purpose is to help each member achieve his goal, every member must take responsibility and assume full accountability for his choices and actions—including those based on recommendations from within the group. Members receive a lot of input from the group, but they are ultimately responsible for the decisions they make. A blamer must be told that he, not the group, is in control of his actions.

Sample comment to address the issue: "I'm sure the other members agree with me—we're disappointed that what we thought would be a good action did not give you the results you wanted. However, it was your decision whether to accept our opinions."

The Attention Time-Sponge

Every member must receive equal attention from the group. The group is responsible to see this is accomplished. An individual may be unwilling to state that he is not receiving his "fair share" of time. Another individual may (even unknowingly) be taking more than his fair share of time. To ensure all members receive equal "attention time," use a timer with a buzzer. For example, each member may speak for a certain number of minutes and the group is limited to a certain number of minutes' response time. When the buzzer goes off, it is time to change.

Sample comment to address the issue: "It looks as if there are some more issues Ted might want us to address. I have captured them in my notes to address at our next meeting. This way, we can move on as we agreed when adopting our agenda."

The Social Butterfly

Mastermind Alliances form close bonds; after all, members are sharing their dreams, doubts, strengths, and weaknesses. While this is powerful (and can be beneficial), it also makes it easy to fall into a social get-together at meetings. The social butterfly is usually outgoing and friendly. It is appealing to chat with this person; however, those conversations cannot detract from the Mastermind Alliance purpose.

The social butterfly syndrome can be countered by designating a "social time," as discussed in Step 7. However, should one member be more inclined to add social aspects during the meeting, the matter should be addressed.

Sample comments to address the issue: "I'd enjoy hearing about your family reunion. May we talk about it after the meeting?" Alternatively, "Sounds like an interesting story, but we should stay on track for the meeting. Let's hold that until our socializing time."

Keep in mind that some Mastermind groups may desire more of a social setting. The group still works toward achieving a purpose, however, it may be secondary in importance, and thus less time is allotted for the actual work towards its goal.

One Mastermind group participant reported such a story. Invited into the group for a specific purpose, she was looking forward to working toward that goal. "I attended several meetings and found they were basically social get-togethers with very limited time devoted to the purpose. I suppose that would have been fine if that was what I was after, but it wasn't."

Asked if she consulted with other members about the minimum amount of time spent on the purpose, she replied, "I did, and they told me they were pleased with the format. I realized that while this group wasn't for me, it was still a successful group in that it pleased its members."

Organization Specific

It is vital that positive teamwork is maintained in the workplace—not only for the organization's success, but for individual success (i.e., people's careers) as well. One cannot succeed in business without the ability to work well in teams.

The potential pitfalls facing a group of people never vary, regardless of the reason it was established or the situation that guides it. While a team comprises individuals, it is also an entity, and all members of the team are responsible for its success. The chain of command should be respected within a business environment; however, members within a team should be allowed more equality of authority to make the teamwork more rewarding to the members, thus more successful to the organization.

When hierarchy rules, dealing with ineffective team members normally falls to the leader. In a Mastermind Alliance, equality allows for any team member to address another member's ineffectiveness, resulting in increased effectiveness and productivity for the group as a whole.

While establishing values/standards of behavior (see Step 4), include the authority for any member to address non-performing members.

Changes

Individuals change—thus the character of groups will change. If the manner in which the group functions, or the frequency or format of the meetings does not produce the desired results, try something different. No meeting structure should be set in stone.

There may be times when a change is needed to the member base of the Mastermind Alliance: an additional member brought in to fill a need of the group or add to its effectiveness. Conversely, a member may not be adding value to the group, and after attempts to resolve the poor performance go without success, it may be necessary to ask the member to leave.

Do not be afraid of change—as the adage goes, "Change is the only thing constant in our lives." It may take several changes to make your Mastermind Alliance its finest, however, when you do...it is magic!

"Risk more than others think is safe.
Care more than others think is wise.
Dream more than others think is practical.
Expect more than others think is possible."
~ Claude T. Bissell

**Mastermind Alliance Quality Checklist**

Mastermind Alliance Quality Checklist

Answer these questions to ensure the quality of your Mastermind Alliance.

1. What is the group's purpose? Will all members embrace it?

2. Who are the members and what value does each one bring to the group?

3. What form of leadership/facilitation will the group have?

4. Will one person be responsible for coordination?

5. Will there be a secretary/recorder?

6. Will a timekeeper be assigned?

7. Will the positions be rotated? If so, how often?

8. What values (standards of behavior) are expected of the group?

9. What is the group's name? How will you use it to promote a sense of team?

10. Where will the meetings be held, when, and for how long? Will those vary? Will some be shorter in length and some longer?

11. What agenda will you follow? Will that vary?

12. How will you stay in contact between meetings?

13. How will under-performing members be handled?

Photo by Chris Campbell

About the Author

NATALIE D. BRECHER is a performance improvement manage-
ment consultant, professional speaker, and trainer on leadership, management, professional skills, and gender issues in
business. She assists organizations in increasing profits by
achieving superior results from their people, and she helps
individuals improve their professional achievements.

Brecher utilizes 26 years of leadership experience as the
foundation for her work. Achieving success quickly in the
field of investment real estate, she has worked with a national developer, two major national syndication firms, and as
asset manager for a lending institution. She has managed a
real estate portfolio valued over $300 billion, with more than
$45 million in revenue.

Managing companies with more than 800 employees
throughout the United States has given her a history of experience in creating successful teams. In addition, her involvement with Mastermind Alliances to advance professional
careers and business development provides strong insight
into the topic.

With 21 years of professional speaking experience,
Brecher has delivered hundreds of keynote speeches and
training programs, instructing participants throughout the
United States, Canada, and South Korea. As well as tradition-

al training formats, her instructional activities include interactive satellite-training and online training via the Internet.

Brecher is a professional member of the National Speakers Association, a member of the American Society for Training and Development, and earned the Certified Property Manager designation from the Institute of Real Estate Management, for which she also serves as a senior faculty member.

■　　■　　■　　■　　■

**To learn about Natalie Brecher's
professional development
keynote speeches and training,
consulting services,
and to find more
professional achievement
educational resources,
go to:**
www.brecherassociates.com

Share the Power of Many

- Benefit when all your Mastermind Alliance members know what is needed to create an effective, successful group.
- Introduce the power of many to colleagues.

To order copies of the book, go to:
www.professionalachievement.com

Books may be available at special quantity pricing for bulk purchases for sales promotions, fund-raising, or educational use.

BOOK ORDER FORM

Profit from the Power of Many:
How to Use Mastermind Teams to Create Success

Mail your order to: Brecher & Associates Incorporated
2209 Curtis Avenue Suite 2, Redondo Beach, CA 90278

Send to: _____

_____

Address _____

City _____

State / ZIP _____

Daytime Telephone Number _____

E-mail _____

_____ Books @ $14.95   Total $ _____
Payable in U.S. Funds Only. Check or money order. No Cash/COD.
For credit card payments, go to www.professionalachievement.com

Ca. residents add applicable sales tax $ _____

Shipping $ _____
US $3.00 per order, plus $1.00 for each additional book
CAN $5.00 per order, plus $1.25 for each additional book

Total Amount Due $ _____
($15.00 fee for returned checks.)

Please allow 4—6 weeks for US delivery. Can./Int'l orders, 6—8 weeks.
This offer is subject to change without notice. (PPMbk1)

This audio CD is presented by NATALIE D. BRECHER, as she shares her knowledge—and lessons learned—from more than 26 years of corporate success and the results of interviews and surveys of professional men and women. Today, a consultant, speaker, and trainer on leadership and management issues, Brecher worked her way from "gopher" to president, learning how a woman can succeed in business...without biceps!

Business without Biceps:
The Untold Truths of Women in Business and How to Make Them Work for You

---

AUDIO CD ORDER FORM

Business without Biceps:
The Untold Truths of Women in Business
and How to Make Them Work for You

Mail your order to: Brecher & Associates Incorporated
2209 Curtis Avenue Suite 2, Redondo Beach, CA 90278

Send to: _____

_____

Address _____

City _____

State / ZIP _____

Daytime Telephone Number _____

E-mail _____

_____ Audio CDs @ $18.95   Total $ _____

Payable in U.S. Funds Only. Check or money order. No Cash/COD.
For credit card payments, go to www.professionalachievement.com

Ca. residents add applicable sales tax $ _____

Shipping $ _____
US $3.00 per order, plus $1.00 for each additional CD
CAN $5.00 per order, plus $1.25 for each additional CD

Total Amount Due $ _____
($15.00 fee for returned checks.)

Please allow 4—6 weeks for US delivery. Can./Int'l orders, 6—8 weeks.
This offer is subject to change without notice. (PPMbk1)

Printed in the United States
88344LV00002B/23/A